WELCOME TO THE GAYBORHOOD!

Listed here are just a few of the infinite ways folks in the LGBTQIA+ community identify. The word "queer" often serves as a catchall for the whole community, though not everyone identifies with the term, so it's always polite to simply ask how folks identify.

SO . . . HOW DO YOU IDENTIFY?

AGENDER

she they

GAY

NONBINARY

VERS

TENDER

Asexual

PANSEXUAL

HE/HIM

DADDY

SWITCH
SWITCH

TIMELINE OF QUEER HISTORY

1900s–1910s

Strict, puritanical religious beliefs and sodomy laws contributed to pervasive intolerance of the LGBTQIA+ community. Queer folks were considered "perverts" or "social vagrants" and were forced to exist on the margins of society for much of the twentieth century.

Early queer activists like Karl Heinrich Ulrichs, Magnus Hirschfeld, and Oscar Wilde brought attention to queer philosophy, identity, and liberation.

OSCAR WILDE

BESSIE SMITH

1920s

The Harlem Renaissance was an explosion of music, art, Blackness, and queerness. Harlem was a hotbed of creative and queer exploration, with icons like Langston Hughes, Countee Cullen, Alain LeRoy Locke, Gertrude "Ma" Rainey, Bessie Smith, and Gladys Bentley leading the charge. Drag balls became popular at this time.

1930s

After Prohibition, gay bars became social refuges for queer folks, though there was still a lack of acceptance for those who lived outside the gender binary and the strict boundaries of homosexuality vs. heterosexuality.

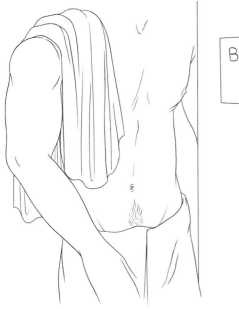

1940s

As the world became more aware of the LGBTQIA+ community in the 1940s, bars were no longer safe places to congregate. This caused a rise of queer house parties and the popularity of "private" public spaces like bathhouses and city parks.

In 1948, Alfred Kinsey published *Sexual Behavior in the Human Male*, the first mainstream publication to address homosexuality in men. Kinsey's subjects, however, were not a good reflection of American society at the time—they were all white men.

1950s

In the wake of the communist Red Scare, violence against LGBTQIA+ folks swelled. The government feared that homosexuality made people vulnerable to communism and deemed homosexuals and other "sexual deviants" security risks. The anti-queer Lavender Scare was put into motion.

In 1950, Harry Hay and a small group of friends founded the Mattachine Foundation—the first well-known organization dedicated to fighting against oppression of LGBTQIA+ folks. In 1955, Del Martin, Phyllis Lyon, and Rose Bamberger organized a secret society for lesbians called the Daughters of Bilitis. Both organizations took a conservative approach to their activism, leaning on assimilation rather than revolution and liberation.

In 1952, Christine Jorgensen became the first widely known American to seek gender affirming surgery. While transphobia ran rampant in mainstream media and gay communities alike, Jorgensen's public experience inspired and validated many gender nonconforming folks.

Christine Jorgensen

1960s

Queer activists began gathering and protesting for equal rights all across the country. LGBTQIA+ folks gathered in bars, homes, jails, at balls, and in the streets to find community, publish queer work, make queer art, and fight for their civil rights.

It all came to a head in the early morning on June 28, 1969, when the police raided the Stonewall Inn in New York City. Five days of riots followed, marking a boiling point in the fight for Gay Liberation.

1970s

One year after the Stonewall Riots, organizers planned the first Christopher Street Liberation Day March. Thousands of queer folks and allies marched up Sixth Avenue and landed in Central Park for an hours-long celebration that is commonly considered the first Pride.

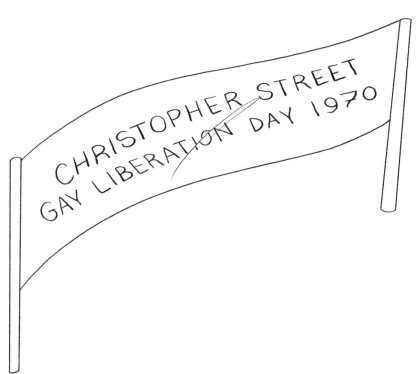

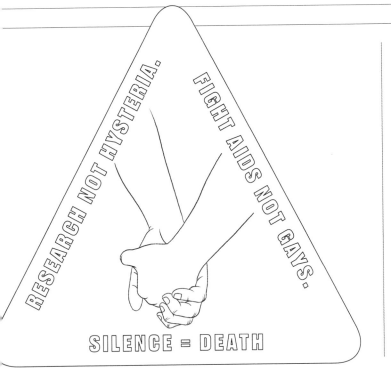

1980s

The 1980s were rocked by the HIV/AIDS crisis. The first case was discovered in 1981; by July 1989, the 100,000th case was reported. With little coverage in mainstream media, queer activists committed themselves to raising awareness of the deadly disease, offering community, and reducing the stigma while rallying for change.

1990s–2010s

Homosexuality was not legally decriminalized in all fifty of the United States until 2003, when a landmark Supreme Court decision— *Lawrence v. Texas*—pushed a group of fourteen lingering states to repeal laws against homosexuality once and for all.

Marriage equality (formerly known as same-sex marriage) was another fight that dominated the political landscape for LGBTQIA+ people in the '90s and early '00s. Marriage equality was legalized in the United States on June 26, 2015.

It wasn't until June 2020 that the United States Supreme Court heard their first case directly regarding transgender rights. The Court ruled that the Civil Rights Act of 1964 extends protections to trans folks, guarding them against employment discrimination based on their gender identity.

WHAT'S YOUR STORY?

Everyone has their own version of queer history to share. What important moments—personal, historic, or otherwise—are on your gay timeline? List them below or go back to the beginning of this rainbow timeline and add your own historic moments.

TODAY'S TAROT READING

Grab your favorite tarot deck, pull a three-card spread, draw it here, and reflect on its meaning on the next page.

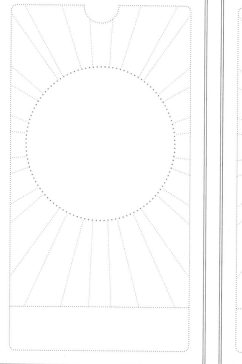

WHAT SHOWED UP IN YOUR READING TODAY?

What themes are present? Are you facing any particular challenges or
celebrating any recent successes? Reflect on the cards here.

_____

_____

_____

_____

_____

_____

_____

_____

_____

_____

_____

_____

QUEER LITERATURE EDITION

Make a list of your favorite books by queer authors here!

MATCHMAKER, MATCHMAKER

Match the LGBTQIA+ icon to their famous book!

JAMES BALDWIN

ALLEN GINSBERG

LESLIE FEINBERG

AUDRE LORDE

ALISON BECHDEL

MAURICE SENDAK

WHERE THE WILD THINGS ARE

STORY AND PICTURES BY

'A pioneering work pushing two genres - comics and memoir - in multiple new directions.'
NEW YORK TIMES BOOK REVIEW

Fun Home
A FAMILY TRAGICOMIC

STONE BUTCH BLUES
A NOVEL

Giovanni's Room

MODERN CLASSICS

SISTER OUTSIDER

THE POCKET POETS SERIES

HOWL

AND OTHER POEMS

Introduction by
William Carlos Williams

NUMBER FOUR

LORRAINE HANSBERRY

PLAYWRIGHT AND WRITER; AUTHOR OF *A RAISIN IN THE SUN* | 1930–1965

HARVEY MILK

AMERICAN POLITICIAN; FIRST OPENLY GAY
ELECTED OFFICIAL IN CALIFORNIA | 1930-1978

GEORGE TAKEI

STAR TREK SWEETIE AND LGBTQIA+
ACTIVIST | BORN 1937

ANGELA DAVIS

POLITICAL ACTIVIST, PHILOSOPHER, ACADEMIC,
MARXIST, AUTHOR, BADASS | BORN 1944

DESIGN YOUR OWN

LOVE iS LOVE

Design your own wedding cake for a queer wedding. Go all out with shaped sprinkles or keep it classy gay minimalist with a chic ombré.

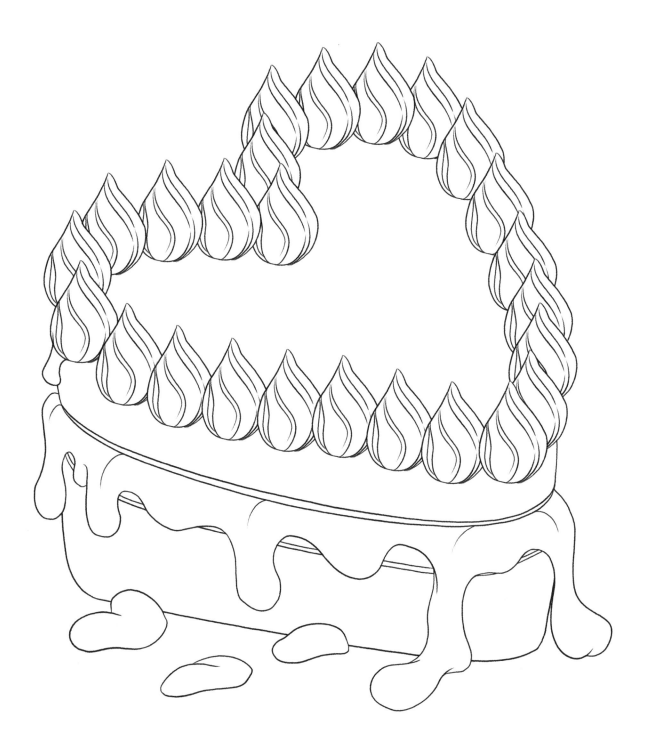

Queer Awards!

It's time to celebrate. Ever wish you could earn a ribbon for the gayest moment of your life? Or give a friend an LGBTQIA+ Lifetime Achievement Award? Now's the time. Design ribbons to commemorate your queerest accomplishments here.

MY QUEER ICONS

Make a list of your queer idols—from history, the media, or IRL—here!

What are your
sun, moon, and
rising signs?

WHAT IS
YOUR
FAVORITE
COMING-OUT
STORY?

WHAT ARE YOUR
LOVE LANGUAGES?

If you could give
one piece of advice
to your younger self,
what would it be?

Describe your worst outfit choice from when you were discovering your ~gay lewk~

HAVE YOU EVER BEEN TO A BRITNEY SPEARS CONCERT? TELL ME MORE

IS THE GAY GLOW-UP REAL?

Whip out your phone, share a pic of your young, awkward self and your current gay hottness, and prove it.

DESCRIBE YOUR QUEER UTOPIA.

WHO WAS YOUR ROOT*?

* The first person—fictional, famous, or IRL—that you had queer feelings for, whether or not you knew it at the time.

DESCRIBE THE WORST DATE YOU'VE EVER BEEN ON.

WHAT'S YOUR FAVORITE PRIDE WEEKEND MEMORY?

RECAST YOUR FAVORITE MOVIE WITH AN ALL-QUEER CAST—GO!

LGBTQIA+

How many words can you make out of the identity labels in LGBTQIA+? Try it!

SYLVIA RIVERA

GAY LIBERATION AND TRANS RIGHTS ACTIVIST; CO-FOUNDER OF
STAR—THE STREET TRANSVESTITE ACTION REVOLUTIONARIES | 1951–2002

CATE BLANCHETT

NOT A LESBIAN, BUT LESBIANS *REALLY* LOVE HER | BORN 1969

LIL NAS X

AMERICAN RAPPER AND QUEER COWBOY
BORN 1999

JOJO SIWA

DANCE MOMS FIRECRACKER-TURNED-
ENTERTAINMENT MOGUL | BORN 2003

Community Quilt!

Quilting with your cottagecore cutie?
Design a collaborative quilt below.

DESIGN YOUR OWN

Denim Jacket

Impress the queer babes in your life with a butch/twinky/dykey/you-name-it denim jacket. Add patches, pronoun pins, and other flair. The jacket on the right is decorated with some ideas to get you started.

MATCHMAKER, MATCHMAKER

Match the gay person, couple, or throuple to their favorite sex toy.

FILL-IN-THE-BLANK DATING PROFILE

You know the drill . . .

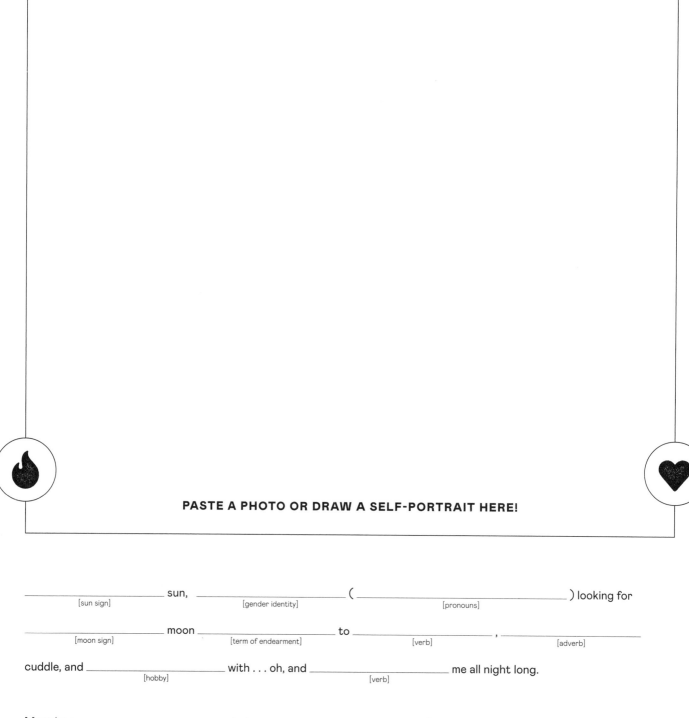

PASTE A PHOTO OR DRAW A SELF-PORTRAIT HERE!

_____ sun, _____ (_____) looking for
   [sun sign]   [gender identity]   [pronouns]

_____ moon _____ to _____ , _____
   [moon sign]   [term of endearment]   [verb]   [adverb]

cuddle, and _____ with . . . oh, and _____ me all night long.
              [hobby]   [verb]

Must love _____ , playing _____ , and _____ memes.
         [queer movie]   [game]   [niche interest]

MATCHMAKER, MATCHMAKER

Match the queer to their animal stereotype!

BEAR   PUP   COUGAR   OTTER

QUEER MOVIES

ADMIT ONE
No.12345

We love talking about the queer canon, don't we? What's on your "favorite gay films" list? What about your "have to watch it!" list?

PAPERDOLL CUTIES

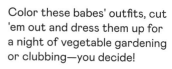

Color these babes' outfits, cut
'em out and dress them up for
a night of vegetable gardening
or clubbing—you decide!

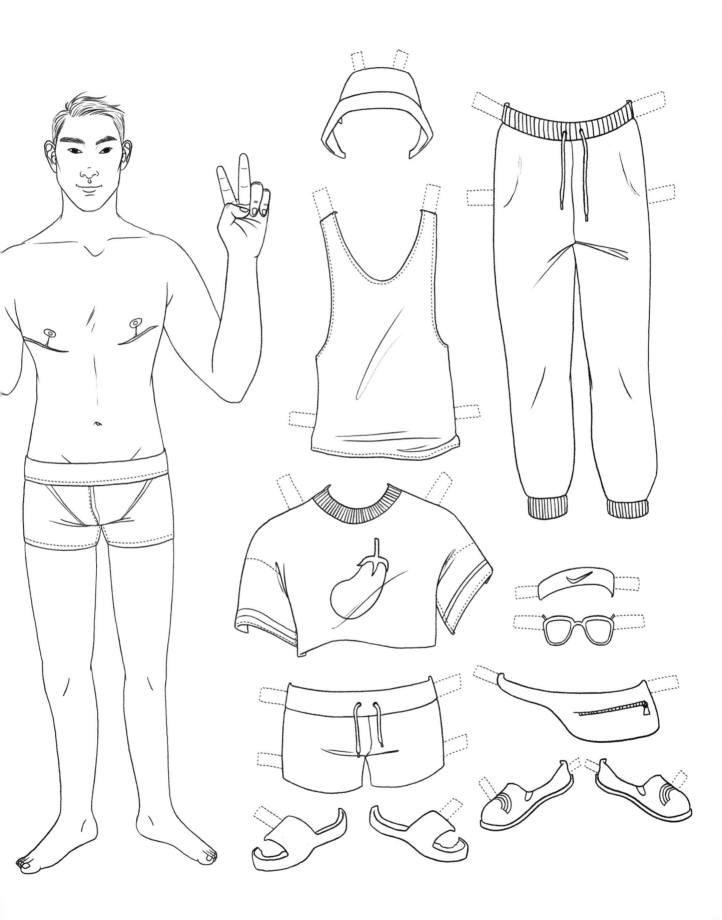

MAKE A LIST
GAY
PLAYLIST
EDITION

Throw together a queer playlist for your next dance party—solo or otherwise!

_____
(PLAYLIST NAME)

QUEER HAIRCUT TIME

This is your chance to flex your hairstyling muscles. Channel your favorite ex-goth, tarot-reading, Sailor Moon–loving pansexual hairstylist. We've offered up some style suggestions to the right, but let your imagination run wild.

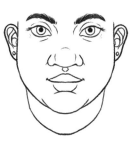

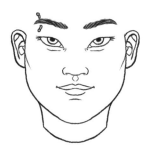

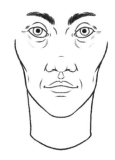

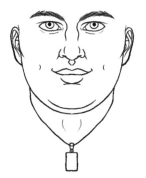

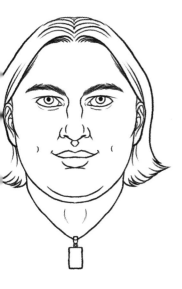

DESIGN
YOUR OWN
T-SHIRT

Who doesn't love
limited edition, small-
batch, anti-capitalist,
support-your-artist-
friends merch?
Design your own queer
tees on these pages.

Tote Bags

Next merch drop goes live in a week! Design your own queer totes on these pages.

Can you spot fifteen differences between the two images here?
Circle them all, then color these queens in!

Tattoos!

You definitely have a folder somewhere of all your tatspiration. Use those images you've collected to design your own tattoos . . . we have some ideas to get you started.

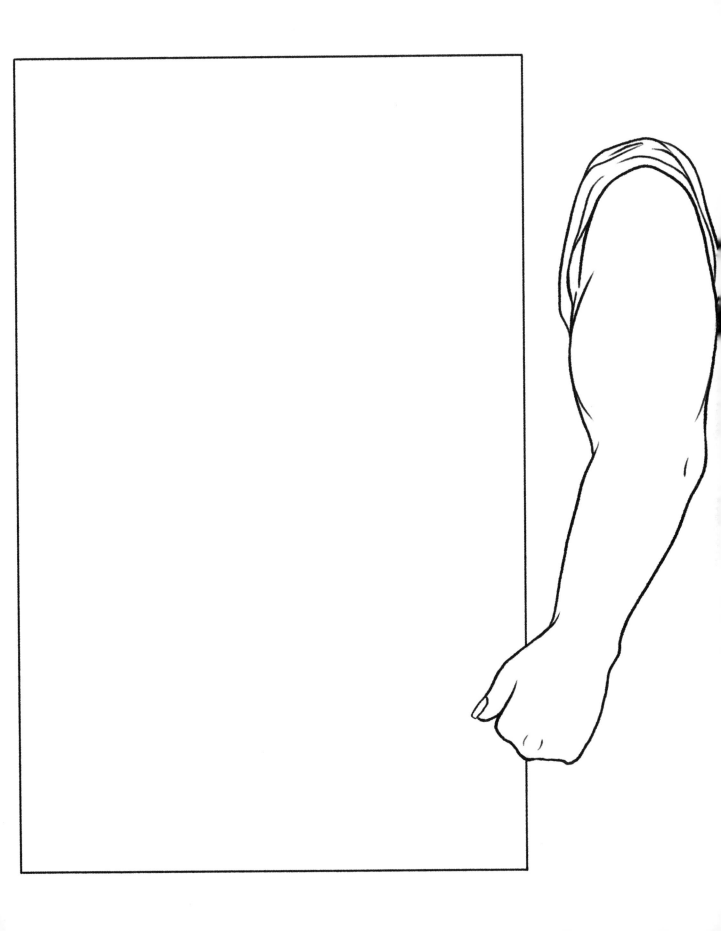

HANKY DOODLE DANDY

Back when it wasn't safe to be out and proud, the queer community developed what is known as the Hanky Code. Colored bandanas—and the pockets in which they were displayed—indicated different sexual acts queers were willing to give or receive.

Color these hankies, add your own patterns, and label them with your own flagging codes. Here's a list of your standard hanky codes, but feel free to get a little freaky.

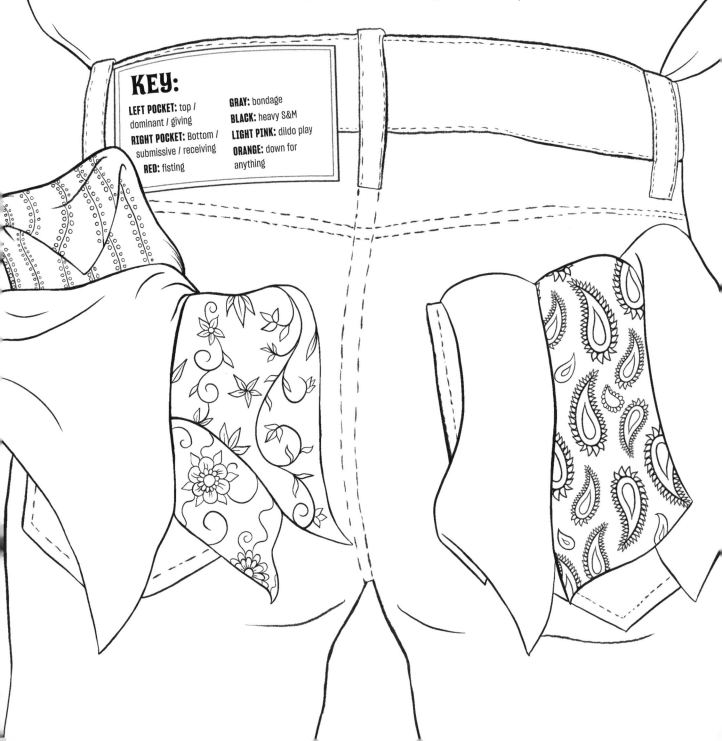

KEY:

LEFT POCKET: top / dominant / giving

RIGHT POCKET: Bottom / submissive / receiving

RED: fisting

GRAY: bondage

BLACK: heavy S&M

LIGHT PINK: dildo play

ORANGE: down for anything

Pride Buttons!

These are just some examples of the buttons queers would pin onto their book bags and leather jackets back in the day. Design your own buttons with punchy slogans.

DIP ME
IN HONEY
AND THROW
ME TO THE
LESBIANS!

Queer
Up!

Pride Flags!

The original pride flag, designed by Gilbert Baker, has undergone a few upgrades since its inception in 1978. Baker's flag had eight horizontal stripes that each represented a facet of queer life. The flag was updated in 2017 by the Philadelphia Office of LGBT Affairs to include black and brown stripes to represent people of color. In 2018, Daniel Quasar riffed on *that* flag and included colors of the trans pride flag.

Design your own pride flags here!

BELIEVE

Black people
Brown people
Indigenous people
trans & queer people
marginalized people
fat people
sex workers
homeless people
deaf and disabled people
mentally ill and neurodivergnt people
survivors
poor & working-class people
Muslim people
Jewish people

UPLIFT

ABOUT THE ARTIST

ANSHIKA KHULLAR is an Indian, non-binary transgender illustrator based in Southampton, England. Their bold and vibrant work, aimed at showcasing the ordinary as beautiful, has garnered them an ALA Stonewall Book Award.

 @_aorists

@aorists